A Gift For:

Cindy & June

From:

Cathy & Paul

Look on pages 29, 39, 40 and 51 for additional
places to add your friend's name.

THOMAS NELSON
Since 1798

NASHVILLE   DALLAS   MEXICO CITY   RIO DE JANEIRO

The Sweet Taste of FRIENDSHIP

KARLA DORNACHER

Published in Nashville, Tennessee, by Thomas Nelson.
Thomas Nelson is a trademark of Thomas Nelson, Inc.

Project Manager: Suzanne Thompson
Editor: Michelle Orr
Designed and Typeset by Brecca Theele

Thomas Nelson, Inc., titles may be purchased in bulk for educational, business,
fund~raising, or sales promotional use. For information,
please e~mail SpecialMarkets@ThomasNelson.com.

ISBN 13: 978~1~4041~9000~9

Printed in Singapore

11 12 13 14 15 TWP 5 4 3 2 1

Most of us are familiar with this little phrase, which is spoken, sometimes even by a total stranger, upon the release of a message. But there's more to a blessing than just words. A blessing is like a beautiful wrapped present waiting to be opened and enjoyed. It is a gift filled with lots of love, good tidings, and promise.

The friendship of others is one such blessing! It comes to us as a gift from God, the blessing~giver of all, and it is wrapped in the heart and life, tears and laughter, and caring and sharing of someone we would call a true friend.

I hope that as you read the words and delight in the illustrations of this little book, you will be moved to celebrate the gift and blessing of friendship.

Bless you,

Karla

THANK YOU

A friend loves at all times.

Proverbs 17:17

You deserve a banner of blessing,
a standing ovation,
a grand declaration . . .

For being a friend so very special,
forever inspiring,
always desiring . . .

to instill within the hearts
of each friend,
a genuine loyalty through
thick and thin.

Dear God,

Thank you for pouring out a drink of Your tender love to warm the heart of my dear friend. I pray for her today that she will receive every drop of blessing You have for her so that her cup is not only full, but that it spills over into the lives of those You've placed along her path.

Bless my friend today with a heart overflowing.

Amen

Savor
This Moment

Apples and Cream Pancake

Have friends over for breakfast and whip up this deliciously sweet pancake.

INGREDIENTS:
1/2 cup milk
2 eggs
1/2 cup all~purpose flour
1/4 tsp. salt
1 Tbs. butter
1/4 cup packed brown sugar
3 oz. cream cheese, softened
1/2 cup sour cream
1/2 tsp. vanilla extract
1 1/2 cup thinly sliced apples
1/4 cup chopped pecans (optional)

In a small mixing bowl, combine milk, eggs, flour, and salt. Beat ingredients until smooth. Heat a cast~iron or ovenproof skillet in a 450° oven until hot. Add butter to the skillet and coat entire bottom. Pour in batter; bake for 10 minutes or until golden brown.

Beat sugar and cream cheese. Blend in sour cream and vanilla. Fill pancake with 3/4 cup cream cheese mixture and top with apple slices. Spread remaining cream cheese mixture over apples and sprinkle with nuts. Cut into wedges and serve warm.

Early Bird Apple Casserole

This is a wonderfully sweet but nutritious casserole perfect to share with friends over brunch.

INGREDIENTS:

2 cups sour cream

12 slices of wheat bread

1 Tbs. butter

12 thin slices of ham
(suggest maple~flavored)

2 cups shredded cheddar/jack cheese

1 cup half~and~half (or hazelnut creamer)

$1/2$ cup packed brown sugar

4 eggs

1 (20~oz.) can of apple pie filling

1 cup granola

Preheat oven to 350°.

Mix sour cream and brown sugar in a small bowl. Chill until serving. Whip eggs and half~and half together. Soak bread slices in mixture. Preheat griddle and add butter when warm. Cook bread on each side until golden brown.

In a 9 x 13 baking dish, place 6 slices of the French toast. Add a layer of all the ham. Top with 1 $1/2$ cups of cheese. Add remaining 6 slices of French toast. Spread apple pie filling over the top. Sprinkle with granola. Bake 25 minutes at 350°. Top with remaining cheese and return to the oven for 5 minutes.

Serve with chilled sour cream topping and enjoy!

You always listen when I need an ear,

You comfort my heart and wipe my tear,

Your counsel is godly,

Full of wisdom, and true,

I thank God for giving me a friend like you.

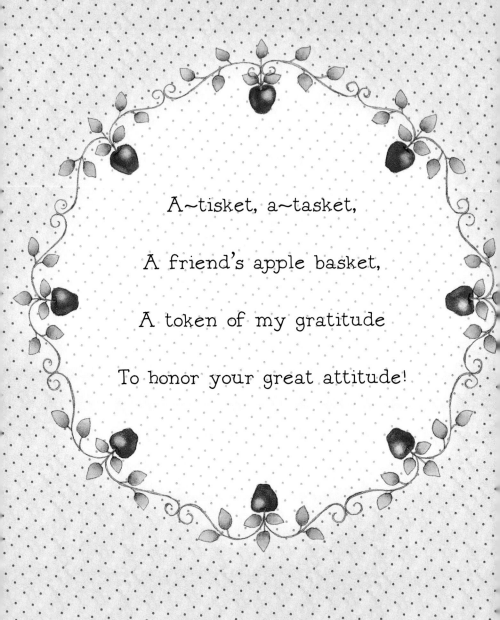

A~tisket, a~tasket,

A friend's apple basket,

A token of my gratitude

To honor your great attitude!

Apple Basket for a Friend

Line your basket with excelsior and add a raffia bow. Start with a few juicy apples and then, depending on the season or occasion, choose a few of the following goodies to finish filling your basket.

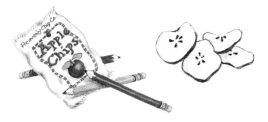

A bag of apple chips
Red and green pencils
Sparkling apple cider
Apple erasers

Dried apples in a bag or on a string
Caramel apple dip with sticks
Apple cider for mulling with a bag of mulling spices

Apple cinnamon tea
An apple~decorated teacup or mug
Apple~flavored jellybeans
A red and green apple towel

An apple parer
Red and green candles
Apple~shaped cookie cutter

Don't forget a little note to your friend that says,

You are the apple of God's eye.

Do unto others as you would like them to do unto you.

Luke 6:31

Respectful
Peaceful
Truthful
Patient
Honest
Kind
Gentle
Joyful
Loving
Helpful
Prayerful
Compassionate

Core Values

A Bushel Basket of Apple Facts

There are tart apples, sweet apples, crunchy and juicy apples. There are pie apples, eating apples, bobbing and drying apples. There are about 2,500 varieties of apples grown in the United States and about 7,500 worldwide, each distinct enough to be given its own name. God loves variety and that's why He created you and me—similar in some ways but very different in others. God made us each unique individuals so that we would bear fruit to meet different needs. Don't ever try to be like me . . . the world needs both of us!

Appleberry Tea

It's easiest to prepare this delightful brew in a 30~cup coffeemaker.

Simply combine the following ingredients and heat:

1 gallon of apple juice
32 raspberry tea bags
16 regular tea bags
1 quart of water
2 tsp. of lemon juice
1/2 cup of sugar

FOR FUN:

If they're in season, add a couple of
fresh raspberries to each cup for a splash of color!

Apple Cranberry Cider

Here is another beverage that is sure to warm the hearts of friends.

In a 5~quart slow cooker, combine the following ingredients:

4 cups of water
4 cups of apple juice
1 (12~oz.) can of frozen apple juice concentrate, thawed
1 medium orange, peeled and sectioned
1 medium apple, peeled and sliced
1 cup of fresh or frozen cranberries
1 cinnamon stick

Cover and heat on low for 2 hours. Discard cinnamon stick and fruit before serving.

Cultivating a friendship garden
requires patience, perseverance,
and time. . . but it's worth it!

SEEDS

FRIENDSHIP
GARDEN

24

Friends
are flowers
in the garden
of life.

The fruit of the righteous is
a tree of life.

Proverbs 11:30

Have you ever thought about how
many apples can grow from a single seed?
One seed, one tree . . .but countless fruit!
You may be only one tree, but your single
life has the incredible potential to impact and
influence not only those closest to you,
but generations to come.

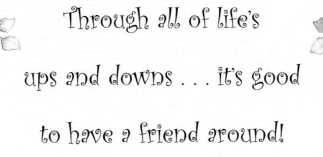

Through all of life's

ups and downs . . . it's good

to have a friend around!

What activities have you enjoyed with a friend?

_____

_____

_____

_____

_____

_____

_____

Dear God,

Thank you for my friend! She is such an incredible blessing in my life. I am so glad that You made her just the way You did . . . right down to the number of hairs on her head . . . and the color of them too! She truly is fearfully and wonderfully made— one of a kind by Your creative design.

I pray for my friend today that You will always enable her to see herself through Your loving eyes—not her own or the world's. Remind her how there is only one of her and only she can fulfill that perfect plan that You have designed especially for her.

Bless her today with confidence in who You've made her to be.

Amen

There's an angel in my garden,
who watches over me,
I know she smiles as I talk to God
under the apple tree.

Thank
you
for
being
a
true
and
faithful
friend.

Hand in hand,
we walk together;
Heart to heart,
friends forever.

Dear friends, you are
my joy and my crown.

Philippians 4:1

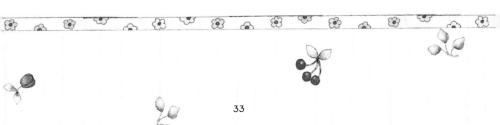

Apple Facts

The average apple contains
5 seeds and 5 grams of fiber.

The first recorded planting of apple seeds was
in 1629 by the Massachusetts Bay Colony.

In early America the apple
was called a winter banana.

The reason we bob for apples is because
twenty~five percent of their volume is air,
and they'll always rise to the top.

More than 3 billion apples are
harvested by hand in Washington each fall.

Statistics indicate that sixty~one percent
of the apples grown in the United States
are still eaten as fresh fruit.

Apples are actually part of the rose family.

The apple variety "Delicious" is the
most commonly grown in the United States.

A is for Apples and Angels . . .

they're both sweet and so are you!

B is for Birds and Blessings . . .

singing the praises for all you do!

good times

crying times

happy times

bad times

laughing times

sad times

A friend loves at all times

12 11 1 10 2 9 3 8 4 7 6 5

Proverbs 17:17 NKJV

giving times

all times!

feast times

receiving times

famine times

Write about a time when a friend
loved you in a special way ~
in rejoicing or weeping.

Fond memories
and a glowing fire
are kindred friends.

Both delight the heart
and warm the home.

Share some fond memories of kindred friends:

_____

_____

_____

_____

_____

_____

Hospitality is opening your

heart and your home and sharing with friends

what God has given you.

42

Kick off your shoes,

Make yourself at home,

Come sit in a comfy chair.

Our lives, our love,

our joy, and laughter,

With you, dear friend,

we gladly share.

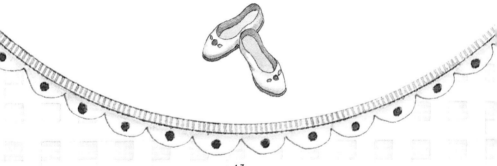

It is more blessed to give than to receive

to~

My Friend
#1 Caring Lane
Tenderheart, USA

Acts 20:35 NKJV

44

HAVE YOU EVER TRIED TO FIND the "perfect" gift to give a special friend? You want her to know how much you care, so you are willing to shop 'til you drop to find it!

To give the perfect gift you must first know the heart of your friend. It needs to fit who she is . . . her personality, her style, her season of life!

Because God already knows your heart, your friends are His perfect gift to you. He knows the need for a proper fit! Consider for a moment the friendships you've enjoyed. Every one has been unique, no two alike. Each one was chosen with great care, by God, especially for you!

He gives us friends, not only for our own blessing, but to teach us to be better blessing~ givers.

Frosted Apple Spice Cookies

Here are fun gifts to make for your special friends!

INGREDIENTS:

1/2 cup butter, softened

2/3 cup packed brown sugar

1/4 cup apple juice

1 cup tart apple, peeled and chopped

2 cups all~purpose flour

1/2 tsp. baking soda

2/3 cup sugar

1 egg

1 cup walnuts

1 tsp. ground cinnamon

1/2 tsp. ground nutmeg

FROSTING INGREDIENTS:

1/4 cup butter, softened

1 tsp. vanilla extract

3 cups confectioners' sugar

3 or 4 Tbs. apple juice

Preheat oven to 375°.

In a bowl, mix together butter and sugars. Beat in egg and apple juice. In another bowl, combine the dry ingredients. Add dry ingredients to creamed mixture. Fold in nuts and apple.

Drop batter by teaspoonfuls 2 in. apart onto greased baking sheet. Bake at 375° for 12~14 minutes or until golden brown. Place on wire rack to cool while preparing the frosting.

For frosting, cream butter, sugar, and vanilla until mixed well. Add enough apple juice to icing to create spreading consistency. Spread frosting on top of cooled cookies and enjoy.

Apple Cake in a Jar

INGREDIENTS:

3 cups all~purpose flour

2 tsp. baking soda

1 tsp. cinnamon

2/3 cup water

2/3 cup nuts, chopped

3 cups apples, peeled and grated

(recommend Granny Smith or Winesap)

1 tsp. salt

1/2 tsp. nutmeg

1/2 tsp. baking powder

2/3 cup raisins

Preheat oven to 325°.

Coat 8 pint~size, wide~mouth canning jars with cooking spray. (Regular~mouth jars also work, but cake will not come out in one piece.)

In a small bowl, mix dry ingredients and set aside. Place water in a large bowl. Slowly add flour mixture from the small bowl, 1/2 cup at a time, and mix well. Stir in apples, raisins, and nuts.

Fill each pre~sprayed wide~mouth jar with 1 cup of cake batter. Bake on a cookie sheet on bottom rack at 325° for 45 minutes. While jars are cooking, heat lids in a small amount of water on stove. Remove from oven one jar at a time. Seal each jar with hot lid and ring.

Decorate the jars by covering the lid with fabric and tie with a ribbon. The cake will stay fresh in the jar for up to three weeks.

A good rule of thumb
is to measure one's
heart with the
yardstick of giving.

Love is a fruit
in season at all times,
and within the reach
of every hand.

♥ Mother Teresa ♥

Dear Friends,
let us love one another,
because love comes from God.

1 John 4:7

Dear Friend,

You are loyal.
You are trustworthy and true.
And no matter what
the cost may be,
I know I can
depend on you.

Share a wonderful memory
of the loyalty of a true friend.

_____

_____

_____

_____

_____

_____

_____

_____

_____

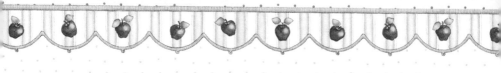

Take a walk down memory lane. . . .

. . . As you pause along the path to enjoy
those special moments from days gone by,
take time to thank God for each blessing and
ask Him how you might give the gift of a
memory to a special friend.

My cup runneth over

Psalm 23:15 NKJV

My friend graciously

serves me

not only a cup of tea,

but also the cup of

total acceptance

and love—a drink

of blessing that

overflows my heart.

Apple Butter Blessings

This recipe is quick and easy starting with store~bought applesauce!

INGREDIENTS:
2 cups unsweetened applesauce
1 1/2 cups sugar
1 tsp. cinnamon
1/2 tsp. allspice
pinch of ginger
pinch of cloves

Combine all above ingredients into a saucepan and bring to a boil. Reduce heat and simmer for one hour. Cool and serve.

For another tasty treat, mix apple butter with sour cream for a fruit salad dressing.

How easy can it be to make a batch and share with a friend!

Apple Enchiladas

Here is another quick and tasty recipe to share as your friends gather around the kitchen table.

INGREDIENTS:

1 (21~oz.) can of apple pie filling
6 (8~inch) flour tortillas
1 tsp. ground cinnamon
1/2 cup butter
1/2 cup sugar
1/2 cup packed brown sugar
1/2 cup water

Preheat oven at 350°.

Spoon 1/4 cup of pie filling evenly down the middle of each tortilla. Sprinkle with cinnamon; roll up, tucking in the edges. Place tortillas seam side down in a greased 2~quart baking pan.

In a saucepan over medium heat, combine butter, sugar, brown sugar, and water. Bring to a boil, stirring constantly. Reduce heat and simmer for 3 minutes. Pour sauce over enchiladas and let stand for 30 minutes.

Bake at 350° for 20 minutes or until golden brown. Serve enchiladas warm with vanilla ice cream. Yummy!

You are the apple of God's eye

58

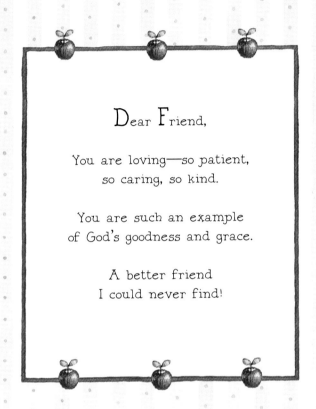

D̲ear F̲riend,

You are loving—so patient,
so caring, so kind.

You are such an example
of God's goodness and grace.

A better friend
I could never find!

I'm so thankful that

God planted you

in my life.

You have added

a beauty and sweet fragrance

like no other ever could.

Romans 12:15 NKJV

May we rejoice in
the goodness
of God
and the gift
of friendship
we have been given.

Every good and perfect gift
is from above.

JAMES 1:17

64

Dear God,

I pray that You will enable my friend to know, more and more every day—how long, how wide, how deep and how high Your love for her truly is—and that, no matter where she is or what she is going through, nothing can separate her from Your unconditional, overwhelming love.

Bless her with Your presence.

Amen

A Bushel Basket of Apple Facts

The smallest variety of apple is the crab apple.
The flowers of the crab apple tree are gorgeous!

October is National Apple Month. That's the
month to look for an apple festival in your area.

One of the very first jellybean flavors was apple.
I wonder if it was a red, golden, or green variety.

The apple muffin is the official state muffin of New York!
Do you think all states have an official muffin?

Moses Coates patented the apple parer in 1803. Thank you, Moses!

Over eighty percent of our country's apples are grown
in only six states. The state of Washington,
where I live, is one of those six.

Sweet Apple Pie

INGREDIENTS:
1/2 cup sugar
1/4 cup packed brown sugar
1/4 cup all~purpose flour
1 tsp. of apple pie spice
6 cups peeled, cored, and sliced tart cooking apples
2 (9~inch) unbaked pie crust
1 Tbs. butter
1 tsp. sugar

Preheat oven to 400°.

Mix together sugars, flour, and apple pie spice in a large mixing bowl. Add the apples and toss to coat evenly.

Spoon filling into prepared bottom crust. Drape the top crust over the pie. Fold the edges of the top crust under bottom crust edge and crimp together with your fingers to seal it. Cut small slices in the top crust to allow steam to escape.

Brush the top crust with butter and sprinkle with sugar. Cover edge of crust with 2~inch stripes of foil. Place pie plate on a cookie sheet and bake for 35 minutes at 400°. Remove the foil and bake another 10 to 20 minutes until apples are tender and crust is golden brown.

Cool on rack. Slice, serve, and enjoy with friends!

Apple Cinnamon Crumb Pie

Try this quick and easy pie recipe when friends drop in unexpectedly to say hello.

INGREDIENTS:
1 (21~oz.) can of apple pie filling
1 unbaked pie crust
$1/2$ tsp. ground cinnamon
4 Tbs. butter
1 $1/2$ cups pecan shortbread cookies, crushed

Preheat oven to 450°.

Pour pie filling into unbaked pie crust. Sprinkle with cinnamon and dot with 1 Tbs. butter. Melt remaining butter. Mix cookie crumbs and melted butter in a bowl. Sprinkle over pie filling. Bake at 450° for 10 minutes, covering edges of crust loosely with foil. Reduce heat to 350° and bake for 40~45 minutes or until crust is golden brown. Cool on rack and dig in.

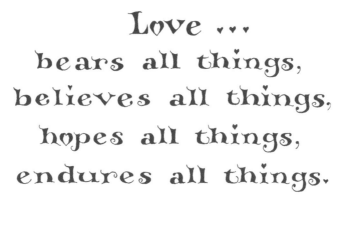

Love ...
bears all things,
believes all things,
hopes all things,
endures all things.

I need friends!
You need friends!
We all need friends!

To speak a word of encouragement,
comfort, or instruction at just the
right moment in time can be as
sweet to the soul and as nourishing
to the heart as a gift of
golden delicious apples
to both the giver and
the receiver.

A word aptly spoken is like apples of
gold in settings of silver.

Proverbs 25:11

Thank you for giving so much to me,
A treasured friend you will always be.

The warm rays of love,

generosity,

integrity,

honesty,

sharing,

and caring

kindle the spark of life

and blessing in the heart

of true friendship.

Seek and you will find.

MATTHEW 7:7 NIV

You are a treasure,
a blessing,
a joy,
a true find!
I'm so glad
our friendship
was in God's design!

• Apple Trivia •

Did an apple truly fall on Sir Isaac Newton's head? It is believed to be true. Amazing that a falling apple would be the foundation of a theory that would change the universal understanding of the laws of gravity!

Johnny Appleseed was born John Chapman in 1774. Yes, he was a real person who earned his nickname not only by scattering apple seeds hither and yon, but by establishing several nurseries throughout Ohio and Indiana. His efforts provided many pioneers with apple trees and encouragement as they settled the Midwest.

According to legend, William Tell successfully shot an arrow through an apple that was perched on the head of his young son. I always thought he was foolishly showing off his skills, but tradition says that it was his punishment for refusing to salute a governor of his time.

Your friendship
blesses my heart

Scatter seeds of blessing

wherever you go. . .

and watch your garden

of friendship grow!

LOVE IS A FRUIT IN SEASON AT ALL TIMES.

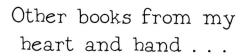

Other books from my
heart and hand . . .

THE HEART & HOME OF CHRISTMAS

KARLA DORNACHER

One of a Kind, by God's Design

written and illustrated by
Karla Dornacher

HeavenSent Baby
A Bundle of Blessings for the New Mom

written and illustrated by
KARLA DORNACHER

For more information on my books and gift products
or to share your thoughts and comments,
please write, email, or check out my website . . . I'd love to
hear from you!

Karla Dornacher 🍎 P.O. Box 185 🍎 Battle Ground, WA 98604
Karla@KarlaDornacher.com
www.KarlaDornacher.com

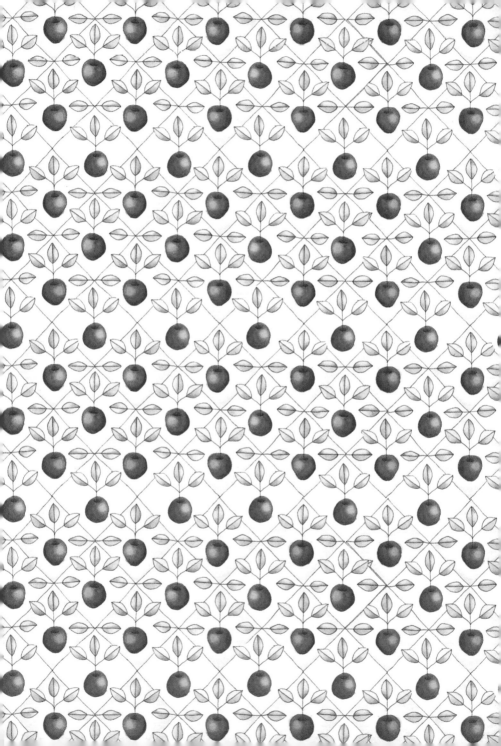